PAYING THE PIPER

Advertising & the Church

A Report of the Working Party established
by the Communications Committee
of the Church of England

*This Report has only the authority of
the Working Party that produced it*

CHURCH HOUSE PUBLISHING
Church House, Great Smith Street, Westminster, London SW1P 3NZ

ISBN 0 7151 3755 7

Published 1994 for the Communications Unit of the General Synod of the Church of England by Church House Publishing

© *The Central Board of Finance of the Church of England, 1994*

All rights reserved. No part of this publication may be reproduced in any form or by any means, electronic or mechanical, including photocopying, recording, or any information retrieval system, without written permission which should be sought from the Copyright Administrator, Central Board of Finance of the Church of England, Church House, Great Smith Street, London SW1P 3NZ.

Cover design by Julian Smith
Printed by Rapier Press Ltd

Contents

		Page
Foreword		1
Preface		2
Chapter One	The Background	3
Chapter Two	What is Advertising?	6
Chapter Three	Some Ethical and Theological Considerations	11
Chapter Four	Codes of Practice	15
Chapter Five	Advertising and the Churches' Strategy	17
Chapter Six	A Church User Group	28
Chapter Seven	Case Studies – Amnesty International, Billy Graham and the Oxford Diocesan Christmas Campaign	32
Chapter Eight	Recommendations for the Churches	47
Appendix A	List of Working Party Members, Terms of Reference and Details of Meetings	49
Appendix B	Independent Television Commission and Radio Authority Codes for Religious Advertisements	51
Appendix C	Useful Contact Addresses	59

Foreword

One of the many changes brought about by the Broadcasting Act 1990 was the removal of the ban on religious advertising on Channels Three and Four television and independent radio. After many years, this has brought commercially-funded radio and television into line with the print media.

This change brings new opportunities for the churches but it also raises a number of questions. Some of these are theological and ethical. Is it right, for example, for a Church whose founder communicated most effectively when he seemed powerless on a cross to use one of the most powerful means of mass communication? And, if the Church uses television advertising, will it not be endorsing materialism and underlining society's urge to keep up with the Joneses?

There are also practical questions of how the use of advertising can be co-ordinated to prevent contradictory messages being transmitted and how to maximise limited resources.

This report does not claim to be comprehensive. It is seminal. Its task has been to identify the key questions which need to be asked about the use of advertising in general, and the use of the electronic media for advertising in particular. It suggests guidelines, first for dioceses in the Church of England and also for consideration by other Churches who are increasingly working together in the advertising field.

I am grateful to Canon Colin Semper and the other members of the Working Party for putting down this first marker.

+ NIGEL McCULLOCH
Bishop of Wakefield
Chairman, the Church of England Communications Committee

Preface

Religious advertising is not new. Churches have been buying space in the print media for many years. The times of services are advertised in the local newspaper without a second thought. Handbills are pushed through letter boxes. Posters are displayed at prime sites; some witty, some gnomic, some using the language of threat or fear which has been pored over for 2000 years. Since 1991, Independent Local Radio has been used to advertise local and regional events. And in January 1993, the Diocese of Lichfield became the first church organisation to advertise on television in this country. Such activity is likely to increase.

As the outlets for communications proliferate, there is an urgent need for the Church to define a clear strategy on the use of religious advertising. To do nothing might open the door to a plethora of unco-ordinated local and regional campaigns and, maybe, to competitive advertising between Christian denominations. In any event, the combined effects of the 1990 Broadcasting Act and the increased use of advertising by the Church means that religious advertising can no longer be ignored.

If advertising is to be part of the communication mix, then there has to be co-operation between Christian denominations in the development of a common strategy. Whilst the sharing of the financial costs is important, Jesus' prayer that 'all may be one...so that the world might believe' is an over-riding theological imperative. The Churches Advertising Network, an *ad hoc* body formed out of the Diocese of Oxford's successful Christmas campaigns, has already set its face against denominational advertising. Evidence from Oxford and Lichfield suggests that denominational messages at regional or national level can have an adverse effect both on ecumenical relations and on the perceptions of those outside the Churches.

So our task has been to ask: 'Should advertising be part of the communications mix and, if so, what might it say and how should religious advertising be monitored to the advantage of the whole Christian community?'

Revd Canon Colin Semper
Chairman of the Working Party

Chapter One The Background

1.1   The glitzy world of advertising has been an integral part of the British way of life for many years. It is a highly professional, multi-million pound industry. It is seen by most people as an essential tool in the marketing of goods and services. Without the revenue from advertising, we would not have the newspapers, magazines and commercial broadcasting which we now take for granted. Because there is no writing of a cheque for commercially-funded broadcasting, there is a feeling it is free. This is nonsense, of course. It is funded by the advertising we pay for through the shopping basket.

1.2   The Churches have been involved in advertising for many years, both as an advertiser and as a beneficiary of advertising revenue. Parishes have advertised in local newspapers and many parish and diocesan publications are dependent on advertising revenue to maintain costs of their publications at a level which is acceptable to their readers. Little use, however, has been made by the Churches of advertising at the national level. The Salvation Army is probably the one major Christian community which has used poster and the print media for national advertising campaigns. On the whole, it has been voluntary organisations, such as The Children's Society, The Catholic Enquiry Centre, Christian Aid and Cafod, who have used national advertising, usually in the print media.

The 1984 Broadcasting and Cable Act

1.3   In 1984, the Government introduced The Cable Act. This provided for the first time in British broadcasting an opportunity for religious groups to advertise. Previous Broadcasting Acts had proscribed advertisements by groups whose aims were wholly or mainly religious. Religious objects, artifacts, even the Bible, could not be advertised.

1.4   A small number of religious groups, mainly American, seized the opportunity provided by the cable Act, including a small group of Christians providing trail-blazing religious programmes on the Vision Channel as part of the Swindon cable system. They decided to transmit some advertisements as part of this service. Equally low-key was the response of the commercial sector. There was no rush to advertise religious products. There was no glint in the eye of ecclesiastical tailors or makers of communion wine. After all, this was 1984 and the number of homes which could receive cable or satellite programmes was very small.

Enquiry Agency

1.5   In 1988, the Christian Enquiry Agency (CEA) was launched with the full support of the major Churches. Although religious advertising was still not permitted by the 1981 Broadcasting Act, the Independent Broadcasting Authority (IBA), in company with the BBC, saw CEA as an agency to whom broadcasters could refer enquiries prompted by religious programmes. The CEA used the print media for its advertisements, which proved a very effective medium in reaching people outside the communities of faith.

The Broadcasting Act 1990

1.6 In November 1990, a new Broadcasting Act came into force. The Government wanted to 'free-off' commercially-funded broadcasting. As part of this, the clause forbidding religious advertisements was dropped. So, religious groups could advertise not only on cable but on ITV and Channel Four. Commercial radio was also opened up to religious advertisements. The Act became effective for radio on 1 Jan 1991 and for television on 1 Jan 1993, when the new regional licences came into force. As far as the BBC was concerned, with the licence fee as its main source of revenue, the question of religious advertising at that point, was, of course, an academic one.

A Code for Religious Advertising

1.7 The 1990 Broadcasting Act required the Independent Television Commission (ITC) and the Radio Authority (RA), successors to the IBA, to draw up and regularly review a code 'governing standards and practice in advertising and in the sponsoring of programmes' (Sec 9.1a). They are also required to prescribe 'the advertisements and methods of advertising or sponsorship to be prohibited' (Sec 93.1a). Both bodies have the power to make different provision in the code for different kinds of licensed services, e.g. for ITV and for cable television. The ITC and Radio Authority sought the Churches' views on a draft code before it was finalised. The Advertising Codes of Practice for radio and television are printed as Appendix B. Both regulatory bodies are monitoring religious advertisements.

The Churches' Response

1.8 Since the 1990 Act extended the possibility of religious advertising to radio and television, a number of Anglican dioceses, one incumbent, a Roman Catholic priest in the West country and a Church of Scotland minister in Glasgow have advertised on radio, and one diocese, Lichfield, on regional television. In 1991, Lichfield Diocese commissioned an advertisement from GRA Christian Radio to draw attention to the celebration of Easter. Oxford diocese used the same advertisement on their local radio. At the same time, the vicar of Jesmond in Newcastle, the Revd David Holloway, placed an advertisement on local Radio Metro reminding listeners it was Easter. These advertisements were followed by an advertisement on local radio by Lichfield in May of the same year about a diocesan celebration at the county showground. Later, Oxford Diocese launched a mini-campaign in December to boost church attendance at Christmas. Radio advertisements were supported by car stickers and small posters. The Dioceses of Derby, Bradford, Ely, Lichfield and Salisbury also used the radio advertisements and the support material. Oxford ran a second

Christmas campaign in 1992. Details of the campaign and an evaluation of it are contained in Appendix C. When religious advertisements were allowed on Channels 3 and 4 in 1993, Lichfield diocese was the first diocese to advertise, buying time in Central Television's western region in January 1993. This effectively restricted the advertisement to viewers in the Lichfield diocese.

Advertising By Charities

1.9 In Sept 1989, the IBA allowed charities to advertise their aims and events. It was argued and accepted by the ITC, that some religious charities' aims were wholly or mainly educational or humanitarian, rather than religious and so should be included in this category. In 1992, they were permitted to solicit donations. A number of charities took advantage of this, including the Church of England Children's Society and Christian Aid.

The Working Party

1.10 It became clear that the Church of England's response to the new opportunities for advertising on radio and television was likely to develop on an *ad hoc* basis without the underlying issues being addressed. In May 1992, therefore, the Church of England Communications Committee asked a small group to consider what the Church of England's advertising policy should be, paying particular attention to ethical and theological considerations. The Church also needed a steer on how to respond to new advertising opportunities and to the setting up of an Advertising User Group.

TERMS OF REFERENCE

1.11 The Communications Committee agreed the following Terms of Reference for the working party:
  i. To consider what the Church of England's advertising policy should be, paying particular attention to ethical and theological considerations;
  ii. To consider the establishment of a Churches Advertising User Group.

MEMBERSHIP

1.12 In determining the membership of the working party it was felt important to include a moral theologian, an advertising practitioner, a representative of a diocese which had advertised on radio, and an ecumenical representative. A list of members is included as Appendix A.

Chapter Two What is Advertising?

2.1   In nearly every newspaper, magazine and periodical, on independent radio stations, on two of the four terrestrial television channels and nearly all the cable and satellite channels, on buses and trains, outside shops, on bus-stops and lining the tunnels of tube stations, there are segments of space and time which can be bought by individuals, organisations and institutions. They pay an agreed rate and, within the boundaries of time and space, they can communicate their own messages about their views, opinions, values or products, directly and on their own terms to specific groups of people they have carefully chosen.

2.2   The messages that operate within these boundaries are called advertisements. Advertising may be defined as any communication which, through the exchange of money or reciprocal favours, is bought by and under the control of the advertiser. Its purpose may be to persuade, to inform, to challenge, or to change behaviour. But it is defined quite simply by taking place within the boundaries of a space which has been bought and is therefore under the advertiser's editorial control, subject to regulatory authority.

2.3   Outside these strict boundaries, messages may be reported second or third hand; they may be praised or ridiculed by the editorial stance of a journalist or the perception of a community; they may be shortened, deformed, abused or altered beyond recognition; they may even be totally ignored. Within advertising space, however, and subject only to the appropriate regulations, the content and quality of the message, its shape, sound, imagery and frequency are under the control of the originator, who can also target the audience with varying degrees of precision.

2.4   Professional communication which takes place outside the boundaries of bought time or space is not advertising and is outside the scope of this report. For example, public relations can create awareness by seeking to influence journalists, members of organisations and the general public by providing information in a range of guises. What happens to that information once it has left the hands of the public relations practitioner is entirely out of his or her control. It is up to the journalist to use it or not and the editor or owner of the medium to justify the cost of the space it occupies. Public relations skills can obtain excellent coverage for a product or an organisation without the need to purchase space but there is little or no control, no guarantee of frequency or even of use, and it is not advertising.

Advertising – The Advantages

2.5   There are considerable advantages to an organisation if it can buy space or time to communicate directly with its chosen audience. It can ensure the message is placed and define the time and duration of its placing. It can select very precisely the audience and choose the media accordingly, define the response it wants and tailor the message to achieve that response. It can ensure that the message is transmitted accurately, without distortion, and it can measure the effects of the message against the all important pre-determined criteria.

Advertising – The Disadvantages

2.6 There are also disadvantages. The market forces of supply and demand can make advertising a very costly exercise when compared with other forms of communication. Whole sections of the media exist on the revenue gained from advertising. Not only is there the cost of buying the space itself but there is also the hidden but very considerable cost of creating the advertisement. The services of an advertising agency are largely paid as commission from the media owner. Then there is the cost of pre-testing the campaign to ensure not only that it creates the desired response in the selected recipients but also that there are no unexpected or adverse responses elsewhere. Finally, there is the cost of following it with appropriate research to discover whether it met the pre-determined success factors.

2.7 So the decision whether or not to use advertising as part of a communications strategy will be, at least in part, influenced by the balance between the cost of the campaign and the expected response. Both can usually be accurately estimated in advance: cost through an agreed budget and response by pre-testing.

2.8 However, the balance of cost against results will not be the only factor influencing the potential advertiser. Competitive factors may also come into play. In today's society, advertising can convey status; and nowhere is that more true than on television, where to advertise is to have 'arrived'. Christian Aid's recent move from the medium of large, outdoor posters (known as '48 sheet' in the trade) to television not only increased its income but enhanced its status as a leading charity. Image and status can also have a restricting effect. Some products, in order to maintain an image of exclusivity, are not advertised in the mass media. So, the decision *not* to advertise can send an equally potent signal.

2.9 Some businesses choose not to advertise for other reasons. One well-known company has chosen to spend its promotional budget on getting its product right and improving customer service. It does not advertise but relies on the customers' word-of-mouth recommendation.

What Advertising Does

2.10 Advertising both telescopes and compresses decision and action into a few seconds, a few words. They are mini-dramas. The themes are legion – good fellowship and friendship, warm family ties and loving relationships between parents and children, success in professional life, pride in personal looks and the anticipation of constant improvement, the accumulation of possessions for comfort and for the minimisation of work, the achievement of social status, the enhancement of personal growth and performance, patriotism and pride in the community, the privilege of choice and the positive values of competition. Yet, despite all this, one of the biggest mistakes people make about advertising is to think that it can sell things. Advertising cannot sell. By inducing a desire for a particular product through the provision of information or the stimulation of envy, greed or jealousy, it can help to create a market into which that product can be sold. By presenting a particular 'image' which associates a set of ideas or feelings with the product, it can make that product more acceptable to a particular group of people or it can change people's perception of the product. It can bring people into the shop; it can persuade them to pick up the product and take it to the till. They may try the product once but, if the product is not to their liking or they discover it is not what they need, they will not be convinced. Advertising can raise awareness of the product and can encourage people to try it. The selling is done by the product itself. What the advertising is doing is to create a 'climate of awareness' within which the product is sold. In short, the advertising prepares the market for the sales team.

2.11   Loosely translated into theological terms, advertising cannot convert people or bring them to faith. People come to faith through contact with an individual Christian or local Christian community. Advertising, if it stimulated people's desire for the holy or motivated them to go to church, could introduce to the local church a group of people who would otherwise not be there.

2.12   This does raise a further set of dilemmas for the Christian advertiser. Using the language of advertising, we might say that while a commercial product may be tailored to meet the needs of a particular market, we have a 'product', the Gospel, which is given to us on trust, to communicate without alteration or diminution. The Church itself might be thought of as a kind of advertisement, created through the death and resurrection of Christ, and the messages we convey through the use of the space we occupy in God's world will communicate more loudly than any campaign. The initiative is God's and the driving force behind our communication with his world is the power of his Spirit. Yet, the differing cultures in which the Church is set will demand changes in the way the Gospel is presented; and the presentation certainly might have a profound effect on the initial take-up of the 'product'. The theology behind the parable of the sower leads us to expect that some will reject the claims of Christ, others will fall away after a while and a percentage of the initial enquirers will continue in faith and membership.

2.13   If advertising assumes consistency of the 'product', and the Church is part of the 'product' being advertised, then this raises problems for a church where, by its very nature, each church and each service within individual churches will vary in a variety of ways. One respondent to Oxford's first Christmas campaign, which encouraged people to 'Wrap up the Kids and bring them to Church', telephoned a diocese to complain that she had taken her two-year-old toddler to the 8.00 am Prayer Book Communion on Christmas morning and found the service not entirely suited to the child's needs! This variability, however, can be turned to the churches' advantage: after all, there is something for everyone.

2.14 What advertising can do is help the churches present a simple, clear message to a large or specific group of people. The nature of the message will in part be determined by the medium which is used. For example, a television advertisement can communicate a fairly complex set of visual and aural messages to a very large number of people but, unless it can lodge those messages in the memory, it is a transitory medium. For this reason, a whole new art form has been developed around the television advertisement using humour, story, song, and expensively created visuals. Equally, a newspaper advertisement can convey detailed information in a different way because it can be read, re-read and referred back to later.

2.15 If advertising can communicate to specific groups of people in specific ways, it can also alienate. Perhaps the best recent example of this was a television advertisement for feminine hygiene products. Following the lifting of the ban on television advertising for certain products, including sanitary towels, one manufacturer invested considerable money in a television advertisement only to find that the advertisement alienated large numbers of people, many of whom complained to the Independent Television Commission.

2.16 Another example of alienation, though of a different order, was the recent Morris Cerullo poster advertisement produced by the agency FCB. In this case, it was the theology behind the advertisements which caused offence to many disabled people, as well as to others. The agency justified the alienation by saying that those it was intending to reach held a theology of healing that was not alienated by the advertising.

2.17 This raises a further question for the Church. Given that some advertisers do not mind alienating certain sections of the community, provided that they achieve the intended response in the selected audience (e.g. recent advertisements by Benetton), can the Church afford to alienate any group in order to reach others? Some church members will object in principle to the use of advertising by the Church. Others may take exception to particular religious advertisements. How far does Jesus' statement that he 'came not to bring peace but a sword' justify the possible alienation of existing members in order to gain new members? Broadcasters have been dividing the audience for years, hoping to build on the audience they keep.

2.18 Advertising, however, can also educate. One of the most successful recent charitable campaigns was Christian Aid's 'We believe in life before death'. Following the 1990 Broadcasting Act, Christian Aid took a decision to move from billboards to television. It pre-tested a campaign with the theme 'empowering the poor'. The pre-testing demonstrated that the phrase was meaningless to a large number of people, so the agency changed the campaign to 'We believe in life before death'. In the first year, transmissions in a test area not only considerably raised the income collected through the door-to-door envelope scheme but also produced a real increase in awareness of the charity's work. Christian Aid has now moved to other television regions and has found a corresponding increase in support.

2.19 For Christian Aid, the advertising campaign was not an end in itself. It was run to support the thousands of people who were knocking on doors as envelope collectors during Christian Aid week and to provide a backdrop to the many talks, sermons and conversations aimed at educating people about aid issues. It was as much about support as it was about education. It underlined the principle that advertising supports people locally but that it can never be a substitute for individual commitment and personal invitation.

2.20 This point was underlined by the Diocese of Oxford's campaign over Christmas 1991 and 1992. Each year, the research after the campaign suggested that, where the local church made effective use locally of the campaign material, congregations increased but, where the local church was apathetic to the campaign, there was less impact on congregations from the wider campaign.

Chapter Three Some Ethical and Theological Considerations

3.1 The final chapter of Eric Clark's informative book on the advertising industry, *The Want Makers*, begins like this: 'Advertising has always aroused fierce passions'. It is 'an evil service', believed Aneurin Bevan. It 'degrades the people it appeals to; it deprives them of their will to choose', thought C.P.Snow. Arnold Toynbee could not 'think of any circumstances in which advertising would not be an evil'. Malcolm Muggeridge prophesied that history would see advertising 'as one of the real evil things of our time. It is stimulating people constantly to want things, want this, want that'. Pope John Paul II has warned young people they are 'threatened ... by the evil use of advertising techniques that stimulate the natural inclination to avoid hard work by promising the immediate satisfaction of every desire.' As for advertisers: 'They exploit human inadequacy', holds Richard Hoggart.

So, advertising is morally controversial. Here are just a few of the claims:

3.2 The power of advertising to mould people's attitudes and affect their spending patterns is often the object of distrust. It is particularly suspect because it appears to work without our realising it, at a subliminal level. People are not necessarily consciously aware of the stimuli to which advertising exposes them.

3.3 Advertising appeals to many undesirable characteristics in human beings. These include anger, covetousness, envy, sloth, lechery, gluttony and pride. Sometimes, however, the appeal is to more positive qualities – love, care for others – but, arguably, advertising encourages the vices more than the virtues.

3.4 Advertising often resorts to stereotypes and can be accused of many forms of 'ism', especially sexism. Women are often exploited as sex objects or typecast in domestic roles.

3.5 Advertising aimed at children targets those who are particularly vulnerable and have limited ability to discriminate. Advertising can excite desires in them which will set them at odds with their parents.

3.6 Advertising of products such as tobacco and alcohol are deleterious to health and can lead to addiction. This has led to restrictions on such advertising in many Western countries.

3.7 Because Third World countries often have fewer advertising restrictions, they are apt to become a special battleground for multinational advertisers and their critics, who object to the aggressive marketing of harmful or potentially harmful products.

3.8 There are shifting lines of taste about what products it is or is not decent to advertise. Arguments have raged at different times over condoms, incontinence aids, haemorrhoid ointments, feminine hygiene products.

3.9 Some advertising is highly competitive between companies. The emphasis is not so much on the positive qualities of a company's product but on what is lacking in the competitor's. In this context, facts are often used in a misleadingly selective way.

3.10 The use of advertising in a political context is frequently subject to the same criticism – among many others. The opposition is derided by misrepresentation; positive policy-making can take second place.

3.11 Undoubtedly, this is a formidable set of criticisms. With the possible exception of the first, however, all are objections to particular manifestations of advertising rather than to the practice as such. Advertising does not have to be conducted in a way which is sexist, appeals to the worst in people or encourages them to buy harmful products. Where advertising is subject to legal constraints and a genuine attempt is made to enforce them, many of these more questionable elements can be restricted and controlled.

3.12 The strength of the first objection, that human beings are relatively helpless in the face of the hidden power of advertising messages, can also be questioned. Many watchers use commercial breaks on television as the moment to make a drink, go to the toilet or take the opportunity for a quiet laugh. People are influenced by advertising but they are also adept at putting up protective barriers against it or filtering it through wit, intelligence and plain common sense.

3.13 The objection may still be pressed by some that, though there is nothing intrinsically wrong with advertising, the cumulative weight of human experience of the phenomenon has been largely negative. Advertising, as we know it, exhibits the marks of a fallen world all too clearly; critics, therefore, claim it is appropriate for the Church to steer well clear of it. But as Christians we should not judge things of this world as being tainted for ever because their past history is dubious. Food that was once sacrificed to idols can be eaten to the glory of God (so runs the main strand of Paul's admittedly complex argument in 1 Corinthians 8 and 10). Christian freedom entails liberation from guilt flowing from past negative associations and a determination to put potentially creative things to positive use in the future.

3.14 In any case, the experience of advertising to date is not all negative. Advertising is often very informative: it provides us with information, in an easily accessible form, which we would rather have than not have. It gives scope for varied forms of artistic creativity. It can be fun. As Clark writes, 'most of us have favourite ads that actually engender affection'.

3.15 However, there are two further objections of a rather more theological nature. The first is that advertising is inextricably bound up with the materialist nature of modern Western society. We have heard the point expressed like this: If the Church is standing out against a consumer society, spending money on advertising would give the impression that it was endorsing the very consumer ethos that it claims to critique. It would compromise the Church and undermine the credibility of its message. This is over-simple. Clearly, materialism is a real temptation and tendency within our society. It is wrong to idolise material goods and judge status in society by possession of them; but many material goods enhance the quality of our lives, so long as we use them properly and keep a sense of perspective about them. Making goods provides people with jobs and an opportunity (to widely varied extents) to be creative; buying them gives people satisfaction and helps to stimulate the economy. Wealth has to be created before it can be distributed.

3.16 Christians who shoot arrows at material goods need to beware of hypocrisy. Do we really regret the advent of the washing-machine which eliminates long hours of tedious labour or the telephone which quickens communication? When a useful product has been made, it is desirable that customers who stand to benefit by it should be made aware of it. Advertising has a crucial role to play in bringing that about.

3.17 Not all advertising is about the selling of products. It is also about imparting important information. For example, the benefits to be claimed under the Social Security system.

3.18 A second theological objection is that advertising commends its products in an aggressive, invasive way. This is hard to reconcile with the teaching of a Master who often shunned publicity, personified strength in weakness, lost his public when he spoke of suffering and described his magnificent obsession, the Kingdom of Heaven, as hidden treasure. In the New Testament, understanding the Gospel is often portrayed as a secret which cannot be unwrapped by mere human stratagems but is dependent on the illuminating work of the Holy Spirit. Paul's description of his sharing the Gospel with the Thessalonians in 1 Thess.2.1-12 emphasises the qualities of gentleness, sharing 'our own selves' and avoiding words of flattery. At first sight, resort to the medium of advertising seems scarcely compatible with such an approach.

3.19 Again, however, this objection cannot be said to be definitive. There is a place not just for the gentle one-to-one approach to sharing the Gospel but for bold proclamation in the public arena. The man who realises the hidden treasure in the field sells all that he has to buy it; both his sacrifice and his joy would be public knowledge. The twin themes of hiddenness and openness are in fact neatly juxtaposed in the New Testament. Jesus gave expression to both when he said (quoting Psalm 78.2) 'I will open my mouth in parables, I will utter what has been hidden since the foundation of the world' (Matthew 13.35). Jesus' habit of speaking in parables had the force both of revealing truth to those who had 'ears to hear' and concealing it from those whose ears were closed.

3.20 Advertising, too, is by turns direct and indirect. It is not always aggressive. With its use of the vivid image, the telling allusion and the humorous situation, advertising is often close in style to the parable. It is not a medium which can be ruled out of order for the Church in principle. Nor is the world of advertising to be shunned. On the contrary, Christ trusted human flesh; the world of advertising, like so many worlds, can be claimed for him. Whether it really is a suitable means of communication for the Church of England to use in the 1990s depends on precisely what is the type of message that the Church is wanting to convey.

Advertising and Ecological Concerns

3.21 Whatever the message, whatever our recommendations, whatever the response, we submit that in any use of advertising by the Church there should always be a consideration of the ecological issues involved. We do not say this in some routine administrative way or because it is now commonplace for reports to be mindful of this area. Advertising produces and distributes large amounts of printed material. Advertising creates the visual impact of poster sites. In radio and television funded by advertising, the growing clamour of sound and vision can be oppressive. Free newspapers and junk mail clatter through the letterbox without so much as a by-your-leave. All these outlets and more raise important questions about the care of the Creator for the creation. So it is crucial that anything the Church does in using advertising should be simple and avoid the lavish consumption of materials and energy which can typify some commercial campaigns. Distribution should follow suit. It would be a horror if handbills were distributed in urban centres only for both message and medium to end up trampled under foot. It would be an equal horror if the Church were to erect huge poster boards on its premises without any regard for the visual impact in a sensitive area. Large billboards erected in the countryside, as in America, communicate more about visual pollution than they do about the message they are intended to convey. By contrast, if the Church were to take a real care about these questions, the message could be substantially enhanced.

Children and Advertising

3.22 Equal if not greater care must be exercised over the targeting of advertising at children. There are currently important restrictions surrounding the use of religious advertising during or surrounding programmes designed for children or where the programmes are likely to appeal particularly to children. Young children have not developed either the critical or protective filters needed to shield them from the direct manipulations of their desires or emotions. After all, most parents will tell their children that 'I want' is not a proper demand. We support these restrictions but would question the thinking that protects children from religious advertising yet continues to allow them to be subjected to intense pressure from commercial advertising. Many of the commercial advertisements targeted at our children carry with them values and assumptions that are in direct conflict with Christian values and are potentially harmful to family life. We recommend that the Board for Social Responsibility, in co-operation with the Board of Education, undertakes further study in this area.

Chapter Four Codes of Practice

4.1 Advertisements have the potential to be manipulative, dishonest and offensive, hence legislation to regulate the advertiser. This is contained in the codes of practice operated by the regulatory authorities – the Independent Television Commission (ITC) and the Radio Authority (RA). The Advertising Standards Authority (ASA) is a self-regulating body for the print and poster industry. A prime concern is for the nature of material to be clearly delineated advertisement or editorial. This means that a medium can distance itself from any dishonest implication that a 'message' is endorsed by the owner, the editor and the journalists. Additionally, a clear signal is given to the consumer that individual judgement must be exercised. In the light of what we have written about children, regulatory authorities have to be alert to the power of advertising over any vulnerable group, guarding the right of such groups to choose freely, without manipulation or undue pressure.

4.2 Equally, it is essential that a religious advertisement should not mislead. Here, the regulators have a problem. If they say, quite rightly, that religious advertisers should not make unsubstantiated claims, does that not rather severely restrict the use to which the Churches can put advertising? The most innocent yet most fundamental of all religious statements, 'God loves you', is by definition an unsubstantiated claim. So, presumably, is the Easter proclamation: 'Jesus is Risen'. God himself is an unsubstantiated claim, in some people's view. It is permissible, however, to deal with this conundrum by making it clear that the advertiser is stating something he believes. The communication of doctrine cannot, however, be the central theme of advertising but must be incidental to some acceptable purpose.

4.3 Those who are tempted to lobby for the removal or re-negotiation of such regulations for radio and television advertising need to be aware of the nature of the door they are opening. How would an advertisement be received which proclaimed that the leader of some cult or other could heal, save or guarantee eternal life? And where can you find an objective measure of what is or is not acceptable? From the religious group itself? On a purely objective view, even the Central Religious Advisory Committee's advice must be seen at one level as 'special pleading'.

4.4 The same problem exists for one other important restriction – that of identification. Quite rightly, the Radio Authority and the Independent Television Commission require that all religious advertisements must clearly show the identification of the advertiser. Thus an advertisement placed by the Jehovah's Witnesses must be identified as such. Where several organisations are involved in the advertisement, the Radio Authority will accept a generic, rather than a specific identification of the religious advertiser, provided the relevant faith is made clear to the listener. For example, an ecumenical Churches campaign was identified as 'on behalf of the Christian Churches'. Yet even this identification could give rise to a future demarcation dispute. After all, who determines which religious bodies can legitimately use the word 'Christian' and which cannot? Do the Christian Scientists qualify? And how about the Christian Spiritualists?

4.5 This working party broadly supports the present tighter framework of regulations surrounding religious advertising and believes that each application for clearance needs to be considered on its merits.

4.6 Copies of the respective regulatory authorities' advertising codes for religion are in Appendix B.

Chapter Five Advertising and the Churches' Strategy

5.1   It will be quite apparent from what we have said so far that advertising is only one element in any communications strategy. Does the Church of England have such a strategy? Do what we might call 'the mainstream Churches' have such a strategy together? Does the Church of England have a clear sense of its own identity and mission? Such is required according to the advertising professionals. What of the longer term? After all, without a long term vision any strategy is likely to have only a short term success.

5.2   In the broadest sense, all church communications should commend the Christian faith and life. So the communications always have to be consonant with the values which the Church professes to uphold. In addition, the methods which the Church chooses to use in its communications speak a powerful message about the Church and what it stands for. The Church must be especially careful not to lay itself open to charges of being manipulative or propagandist.

5.3   Moreover, in a world increasingly impatient of religious disputes and divisions, the extent to which the Churches are seen to be collaborating to tell a common message is another important act of communication. The more that Churches develop their own distinctive ways of communicating with the public, the more easily are Churches seen as competitors and not as partners in a common witness. Yet this is a very real difficulty because Churches acting together tend to have problems establishing a clear identity in the public mind. Those responsible for developing church communications strategies, therefore, need to give more attention to ways in which Churches communicating on an ecumenical basis can sharpen their public image and convey their message in more attractive and compelling ways.

5.4   The ecumenical aspect of church communications is becoming increasingly important for practical reasons, too. The costs of using certain media and forms of communication, not least advertising, are often too great for all but the largest and best endowed churches. In addition, churches can share each others' skills and expertise in all areas of communications, from church newsletters to broadcasting. What is said about inter-church relations also needs to be emphasised *within* churches. Dioceses, parishes and church organizations belonging to the same Church need to share resources and expertise, too, if they are to increase their effectiveness and sustain their communications efforts over the long term.

5.5   Finally, and it may be unfashionable, Churches need to think hard to sustain their communication. They should be suspicious of pre-packaged thinking designed for, say, the video cassette machine. A brief flurry, the one-off campaign, these are no substitutes for the hard graft of learning to communicate effectively at all levels of church life. If this work is to be sustained and improved, any church must know precisely what resources are available, be they intellectual, financial, personnel or technical. That is why any communications strategy needs to know what already exists by way of resources, structures and activities. Not another audit! Yes. It is necessary. We doubt that even those working in Christian communication in one church would know the details of how another church operates: and they should. Without such knowledge the place of advertising cannot be properly determined.

5.6 These are important structural matters but more important is the necessity to stand back and ask the basic questions. For example, if there is to be an advertising campaign, what would we like to achieve? Is this a realistic aim? So far as it is in us to determine, can advertising deliver the result? Can we provide enough resources to do the job properly? Might we do better to try another way which could be as effective or more so?

5.7 It is beyond our remit to provide a training manual. After all, there are advertising agencies. The Institute of Practitioners in Advertising can supply a list. The agencies have show reels of their commercials and campaigns. However, we suspect that the cost of an agency may be beyond most churches.

5.8 The network of Diocesan Communications Officers may be able to help because, even though the skills and experience of individual DCOs may not include advertising, they may well know of advertising professionals who are worshipping members of local churches and who would be only too pleased to offer help and advice.

5.9 We cannot provide a training manual for would-be advertisers. We cannot provide a manual for would – be constructors of a communications strategy. What we can do is to provide a sort of checklist for any strategic compilation.

Elements of a Communications Strategy

5.10 When thinking about a communications strategy, a church, like any organization, needs to:

(1) identify the public(s) it is trying to reach;
(2) clarify the purpose(s) and desired result of its communication;
(3) choose the appropriate channel(s) of communication;
(4) choose the appropriate forms for its message(s);
(5) formulate the message(s);
(6) communicate the message(s);
(7) evaluate the effectiveness of its communication

PUBLICS

5.11 A church may want to reach one or more of the following publics:

(1) regular churchgoers;
(2) occasional churchgoers;
(3) the lapsed;
(4) non-churchgoers;
(5) the general public in a local community;
(6) the general public;
(7) specific groups (e.g. clergy, young people, young families, old people, local councillors, politicians, newspaper editors, etc, etc).

The size, composition and characteristics of a public need to be considered carefully. The more precisely a church can define its publics, the more effectively can it direct the right kind of communication to them.

PURPOSES OF COMMUNICATION

5.12 Having identified the public or publics it wishes to reach, a church needs to decide more precisely what it wishes to achieve in its communications. It may wish to do all or some of the following:

(1) inform people about or raise their awareness of its (or other groups and organizations') existence, activities, beliefs or practices;
(2) educate people about religion generally or about particular doctrines, views and opinions;
(3) persuade people to change their behaviour or beliefs; to convert, to join a particular church or organization; to give money; to attend church or come to particular events.
(4) instruct people in their faith.

CHANNELS OF COMMUNICATION

Media Selection

5.13 The selection of appropriate media will depend not only on the available budget but on the message to be communicated, the selected target audience, the campaign strategy and the ethical and religious stance taken by the medium itself. The key decisions will depend on using the media which will reach the selected audiences most effectively. The options fall into several clearly defined categories. Many of these are already being used effectively by the Churches.

5.14 When the public and the purposes have been identified, a church has then to consider the various available channels of communication:

(1) personal channels of communication —
face-to face, letters, telephone, fax;

(2) impersonal channels of communication —
display media: noticeboards, special displays, posters
literature: leaflets, pamphlets, brochures, newsletters
AV media: photographs, slides, audio tapes, video tapes;

(3) mass media channels of communication —
books, newspapers and magazines; national and local radio and television, teletext, cable television.

5.15 These channels have then to be considered for their suitability in meeting the church's communication objectives. The channels have to be evaluated according to the following criteria:

(1) Accessibility —
how accessible is the channel to the public being communicated with?

(2) Ease of use —
how easy is it for the public to use this channel?

(3) Response potential —
how quickly and easily can the public respond to communication through this channel?

(4) Addressability —
how easy is it to address messages to particular individuals/groups through this channel?

(5) Capacity for complexity —
can this channel easily convey complex messages?

(6) Message capacity —
how many different messages can be sent through this channel?

(7) Confidentiality —
can confidential messages be sent through this channel?

(8) Formality —
how formal or informal is this channel?

(9) What proportion of the target audience uses the channel?

(10) Browsability —
how easy is it to browse for particular messages in this channel?

(10) Ease of transmission —
how easy is it for the message sender to use this channel?

(12) Time and space constraints —
do senders and recipients need to occupy the same time and/or space?

(13) Control over reception —
does the sender or the recipient exercise more control over the time when the message is received?

(14) Cost —
how much does it cost to use this channel?

(15) Ease of evaluation —
how easy is it to evaluate the effectiveness of this channel?

Applying these criteria will help establish which channel or combination of channels is likely to be of most use in reaching the target public or publics.

MESSAGE FORMS

5.16 At the same time that the channel or channels of communication are being identified the forms in which messages can be cast have to be considered. Message forms include:

(1) Personal communication channels
    Conversation
    Speech/presentation
    Story

Sermon/homily
Performance
Personal letter
Personal fax

(2) Impersonal communication channels
Display media
Picture
Slogan
Poster advertisement
Literature
Information leaflet
Publicity brochure
Advertising flyer
Display/classified advertisement in magazine/brochure
Cartoons
AV media
Still pictures
Sequence
Music/song
Recorded speech/talk/meditation/story
Video documentary/magazine/drama/talk/story

(3) Mass media channels
Press
Feature article
Editorial comment
Regular/occasional column
News story
Interview
Photograph
Display/classified advertisement

Radio, tv and cable
News story
Documentary
Interview
Talk
Worship
Drama
Entertainment
Spot advertisement

5.17 As with the channels of communication, the message forms have to be assessed for their suitability. Many of the same criteria used to evaluate the channels can be used to assess the message forms.

(1) Addressability —
how easy is it to address messages to particular individuals/groups through this message form?

(2) Ease of understanding —
how easy is it for message recipients to understand messages in this message form?

(3) Capacity for complexity —
can this message form easily convey complex messages?

(4) Formality —
how formal or informal is this message form?

(5) Credibility —
how credible is this message form?

(6) Ease of production —
how easy is it for the sender to produce messages in this message form?

(7) Cost —
how much does it cost to use this message form?

(8) Long-term impact —
what is the likely long-term impact of this message form?

(9) Ease of evaluation —
how easy is it to evaluate the effectiveness of this message form?

MESSAGE FORMULATION AND PRODUCTION

5.18 Having identified audiences, purposes, channels and message forms, a Church is now in a position to finalise the messages or set of messages which will meet its communications objectives.

EVALUATION

5.19 Evaluating the effectiveness of a communications strategy can be difficult for a church or any organization working with limited budgets. Elaborate audience research studies are probably out of the question in most instances.

Nevertheless, churches should try as far as possible to find ways to monitor and evaluate their communications activities. The more precisely targeted the communication, the easier it is to monitor and evaluate its effectiveness. It is relatively simple, for example, to devise a system for evaluating the success of direct mailings from a specified group asking for support or money.

5.20 Some measure of the effectiveness of a communications activity, for example, an advertising or public relations campaign, can also be obtained by comparing information about attendance or enquiries from before and after the campaign. Such information, however, needs to be treated with caution, as it is generally difficult to demonstrate a causal link between specific communications activities directed at sections of the general public and changes in the behaviour of individuals or groups. The extent and sophistication of the research methods used to evaluate the campaign need to be carefully considered.

WHICH FORM OF ADVERTISING TO USE?

5.21 The decision on which medium to use for advertising will depend not only on the budget available but on the message to be transmitted, the selected target audience, the campaign strategy and what is permitted by the advertising code. Primary among these considerations is which one will be most effective in reaching the target audience. There are several options, some of which are already used by the Churches.

Newspapers

5.22 Many churches are already using local newspapers to advertise the times of their services. During religious festivals and missions, other messages are advertised. Newspapers have several advantages for the Church. First, they usually have a readership which can be defined both geographically and socially. Second, they can be read and re-read, picked up, put down and referred back to later. Third, fairly complex messages can be printed using both words and pictures. The Christian Enquiry Agency uses newspapers and magazines very effectively and finds that the response from some of the national newspapers is good. Additionally, on the principle of self-interest, it is usually possible to obtain editorial coverage of an event advertised in that newspaper!

5.23 At a local level, there is usually a choice between a paid local or regional newspaper and the plethora of free newspapers. Local knowledge will usually help the decision but budding communicators should be careful to check claims made by free newspapers about their reach and their effectiveness. They should also remember that the price of advertising space is open to market forces and, as with many commercial deals, negotiation can reduce costs. The Diocesan Communications Officer should hold lists of local and regional newspapers, trade press and local magazines and should be able to advise.

Posters

5.24 Posters can be highly effective. They can range in size from A5 to the more specialist 20ft x 10ft (48 sheet) outdoor posters. They can convey simple, clear messages to large numbers of people. The visual impact is as important as the wording and poster creation is a specialist art form in itself. The potential for major poster campaigns is dramatic because most churches own a considerable amount of space on which temporary poster sites can be erected and many have existing site space available at low cost or free of charge. Poster campaigns can have a big impact and, by comparison with television, are not too expensive to run and can be placed accurately in most communities. They are, however, largely urban creatures.

Independent Radio

5.25 Apart from the national outlets Classic FM, Virgin and Atlantic 252, independent radio is all regional or local. Making a successful radio advertisement requires specialist skills but local churches should not be put off using this medium. It can be relatively cheap, it can reach a huge audience, most of whom are not keen churchgoers, and it can be used in conjunction with a telephone number for further information. Although the station may reach a geographical area much wider than the needs of a particular church, if the advertisement is worded so that it is only applicable to 'town A', people in other towns or areas will 'filter' the information and disregard what is not relevant. The local radio station's advertising department can provide advice and a rate-card (which will nearly always be negotiable) and independent advice on creating and using radio advertisements may be obtained through the Diocesan Communications Officer or a commercial advertising agency.

Television

5.26 It is possible that television is still the most powerful advertising medium. We say 'it is possible' because several professionals warned us about being ensnared by television and by hasty assumptions. Television advertising costs big money. It has reach and potency: but time and again we were warned that it would be foolish for any organisation to plunge in without the most careful thought, research and pre-testing. If the Church of England were to advertise itself, time and again we were directed to consult other denominations and to think deeply about what was being said and about the likely effect of any campaign, whether its purpose was to increase church attendance or illuminate, say, some aspect of the work of God in Christ.

5.27 The exception to this is specialised religious channels. Where they exist, religious bodies may use them for advertising with fewer restrictions than on the other channels. In fact, they can be used much in the same way as local independent radio.

Cinema

5.28 Cinema advertising can also be a very effective medium, is not as expensive as people imagine and can reach a selected audience, particularly in the 16/34 age range. It can be used locally and the usual advice should be sought.

Displays and Exhibitions

5.29 Displays and exhibitions can provide a useful form of advertising though, to be done well, they need large amounts of energy and money and, because of the physical difficulties involved, they are not a medium that necessarily comes at the top of the list when thinking about the use of resources for communication.

Direct Mailing

5.30 Direct mailing is used extensively by national charities to maintain and build membership, to encourage member loyalty and to increase revenue. Such is the glossy nature of much of what comes through our letter boxes that direct mailing might intimidate the small operator. This should not be so. After all, leaflet distribution has been a part of the Christian armoury for a long time and we can see that direct mailing could be an effective way of holding and building fringe members.

Support Material

5.31 Most advertising campaigns need some form of support material. For example, if a response is needed then a mechanism of response is required. In an independent radio advertisement, a telephone number can be given and an answering machine provided to collect names and addresses. A coupon is common place for newspapers.

Freepost Licence

5.32 It came to our notice that a number of churches have experimented with buying a freepost licence from the Post Office at a cost of around £90. In this way, a freepost response coupon can be included in leaflet drops. One church uses this effectively to offer free copies of the Lion pocketbooks to enquirers. The Christian Enquiry Agency has considerable experience of the response coupon.

5.33 The telephone is a key support medium. The provision of recorded information can solve the problem of what to do when there is a slightly complex or lengthy amount of information to make available to a large number of people. A simple advertisement with a prominent telephone number, either manned or connected to a pre-recorded message machine, can be a highly effective way of communicating. Beware, however, of using a private individual's telephone number because, once the campaign is over, it can be annoying to continue to receive telephone calls and, during the campaign, the number can be tied up to the annoyance of the owner. British Telecom can provide an 'incoming calls only' telephone line for around £19 a quarter and it is far better to purchase a dedicated telephone line for a campaign.

ADVERTISING AND PUBLIC RELATIONS

5.34 We have been told that one benefit of running an advertising campaign is the amount of general interest and free publicity that it can generate. Whilst recognising this interest, it does not in our view substantiate on its own the mounting of an advertising campaign. A good advertising campaign can be reinforced by PR. We strongly recommend that such PR is carefully managed and, as far as possible, maintained within a pre-defined campaign strategy.

5.35 We are particularly concerned about the use that an advertising agency might make of a campaign it is running on behalf of a church or religious group. We advise that it is made clear to any agency employed by or working for a church that it should not use the relationship for the benefit of the agency, either through its own advertising or in its client list. Client lists should be checked before an agency is hired to make sure they do not contain clients whose purposes may be in conflict with the teaching or principles of the church. A list of useful addresses appears as Appendix D.

Chapter Six   A Church User Group

6.1   Our terms of reference specifically asked us to consider the establishment of a Churches' Advertising User Group. We have therefore given consideration to the following:

   (a)   what exists at present;
   (b)   the purpose and task of such a group; and
   (c)   a possible structure for a user group to achieve the task we have identified.

What Exists at Present

6.2   Apart from commercial organisations supplying pro-forma advertising and publicity materials to churches (such as the Christian Publicity Organisation, based in Worthing), there are currently two organisations which exist within the structures of the Church and which are primarily concerned with advertising

6.3   The first is the Christian Enquiry Agency, founded in 1988 at St Bride's, Fleet Street, but currently located at Inter-Church House. Under the direction of the Revd Tony Beetham, its original purpose was to place advertisements in the national press to attract enquiries about the Christian faith and to provide a response mechanism for those enquiries. It has recently allowed its response mechanism to be used by churches and has developed a range of reply-paid response cards which achieved more than half its total enquiries in 1992. It is also co-operating with the Board of Mission in developing designs for leaflets for use at weddings, funerals, baptisms, Christmas and Easter services and to welcome visitors to churches. It achieved 2,000 enquiries in 1992, of which 37 per cent were men aged between 21-40. Within this context, we see its purpose as primarily evangelistic, although there is no doubt that it has built up a body of experience in advertising which is of great value to the church.

6.4   Its 1992 annual report says: 'The future of the Agency is still threatened by lack of regular funding. Despite encouraging things said about the CEA by church leaders and the media, actual funding for its potential outreach ministry is often not forthcoming.' It received only £12,500 from the main supporting denominations in 1992. We believe that the work of the CEA should be seen as an integral part of the communications strategy for the Churches. We therefore recommend that it be more fully integrated into the mainstream activity of the Churches, and fully represented on any mechanism established to co-ordinate advertising activity.

6.5   The second organisation is the informal ecumenical network brought together after the Diocese of Oxford's first Christmas campaign in 1991 was taken up by other dioceses and denominational regions. The idea for such a group was first expressed in a paper to the Church of England's Communications Committee dated June 1991 after a discussion between the DCOs of Coventry, Winchester, Lichfield and Oxford and the Director of the Christian Enquiry Agency, Tony Beetham. It followed the first advertisements on independent radio before Easter of that year and said: 'We have the possibility of a major, co-ordinated advertising campaign by the Churches using high-profile media. Yet we have no formal group holding the brief either to pray over, think about or research the issues, or to co-operate with independent financial groups or other denominations'.

6.6 The paper also expressed the following concerns:

> (a) '...that there should be some forum for the exchange of experiences and resources, and possibly some form of group buying, so that, by clubbing together, more could be made of available resources',
>
> and
>
> (b) 'without such a group, we might be more at the mercy of independent advertising campaigns than we had previously realised'.
> (Paper written June 1991)

6.7 From those small beginnings, this informal network has grown as the forum within which the Christmas and Easter advertising campaigns are planned and owned. Co-ordinated by the DCO for Oxford Diocese, the Churches' Advertising Network has been meeting about three times a year and has a fluid membership of regional representatives participating in the Christmas campaigns and, more loosely, of non-participating representatives who, none the less, want to keep in touch with developments.

The Task for a Users Group

6.8 In any commercial or industrial organisation and in all major charities, great care is taken to ensure that any message conveyed by advertising, and all major advertising campaigns, are agreed by a properly authorised person, usually at board level. It would be unthinkable, say, for the local manager of a national car dealership to run a regional advertising campaign on radio or television on his own authority. We asked Christian Aid what their attitude would be towards a regional organising group that wanted to fund an advertisement of their own creation for the charity. The response was simple: 'We would not allow it'.

6.9 The reason for this level of control is that great care is taken over the cohesion, the integrity and the image of the company or charity and also, of course, about the messages that are conveyed. As we have emphasised time and time again, not only do those messages need to be properly researched and agreed but the campaigns need to be part of a consistent long-term, well-considered strategy. Yet the Church faces the difficulty that, at the moment, each denomination and each region within each denomination may properly authorise campaigns within their region. We believe that the combined effect of running different campaigns with different aims and messages, possibly at overlapping times within the same geographical area, will be to communicate confusion, signal a waste of resources and work to the detriment of the Church's mission.

6.10 We believe that the Church has to face this issue firmly and provide an appropriate mechanism to authorise and agree proposed advertising campaigns. That mechanism itself needs clear guidelines and appropriate supporting authority to determine the level of activity at which national agreement becomes necessary and the level of research and professional advice required before a campaign is executed. It would be inappropriate, for example, to require national agreement for an advertisement for a church fete run on one local radio station. It would be just as inappropriate, however, for a single diocese to commission and execute a major campaign without such national agreement.

6.11 The issue becomes more acute, and certainly more complex, when the proposed campaign is ecumenical. In today's welcome climate of ecumenical co-operation, however, it is hard to envisage any single denomination commissioning and executing a national or major regional campaign without consulting its ecumenical partners and taking note of their advice or concerns. We welcome the strong emphasis on ecumenical co-operation that has been a hall-mark of the recent Christmas advertising campaigns and suggest that any mechanism adopted should continue this ecumenical approach.

6.12 It is clear from the recent history of the Churches' involvement in advertising that it is an evolutionary process and that there is a willingness amongst the denominational Churches to co-operate on an ecumenical basis. There may be times when individual denominations may wish to advertise their work or reinforce their particular identity but we believe that the establishment of an inter-denominational consultative body, far from preventing individual initiatives, would strengthen understanding between us.

6.13 We therefore recommend that an inter-denominational consultative body for religious advertising is established at national level, owned and formally authorised by those denominations wishing to participate.

6.14 Such a body would:

(a) act as the focus of a network co-ordinating the advertising activities and aspirations of the participating denominations;

(b) relate structurally to the denominations participating in the network to ensure that campaigns are consonant with the wider communications strategies of the participants;

(c) reflect theologically on every aspect of proposed campaigns to ensure that they are consonant with the mission and teaching of the Church;

(d) have powers to ensure that extraneous, conflicting or inappropriate campaigns or messages are not run;

(e) raise and hold funds from denominational and other sources both for administration and for specific campaigns;

(f) ensure the most efficient use of available resources by sharing costs and resources.

6.15 It might also be available to be consulted by those responsible for regulating religious advertising and would provide a pool of expertise for anyone wanting advice or support for a local initiative.

6.16 It was partly to meet these concerns that, in the absence of an existing structure, the Churches' Advertising Network was formed. It is not part of any formal ecumenical instrument and operates by mutual agreement of its members. It has, to borrow a phrase from the 1990 Broadcasting Act, 'a light touch' and has been able to respond quickly, professionally and creatively to the opportunities presented by that Act. It has developed, over a relatively short period, a considerable pool of expertise.

6.17 We have said that the Church should firmly grasp the issue of control and authorization and have suggested a mechanism to this end. Provided that participating denominations agree to submit proposed campaigns to the consultative body, we believe that this process can be achieved in a way that is entirely consistent with the structures of dispersed authority in the Churches. Comments, suggestions or reservations from the consultative body can be fed back to the proposer and, if the consultative body is seriously concerned about any proposal, they would have the discretion to make their concerns known to the proposers' bishop or church authority. Such a process would stimulate a two-way process of discussion and learning, rather than being overly authoritarian.

6.18 We recommend that this consultative body be appropriately funded to enable it to carry out these functions through a budget drawn up and agreed with participating denominations.

6.19 We also recommend that it have the power to raise and hold funds from participating denominations and other supporting bodies for particular campaigns.

6.20 We therefore recommend that the model that has been developed thus far should be endorsed and strengthened in the ways we have suggested and in a way that protects its creativity and enterprise from an overly bureaucratic structure.

Chapter Seven   Case Studies

7.1   Carolyn Woolrich from FCB and Richard Thomas, DCO for Oxford Diocese, provided case studies respectively of campaigns for Billy Graham and Oxford Diocese. Marilyn Sweetland also drew the Working Party's attention to a campaign by BMP for Amnesty International, which is published with their approval. All three campaigns illustrate, in varying degrees, the principles required for an effective campaign.

Case Study: Amnesty International 1988 - 1990
Advertising Agency : BMP

7.2   Amnesty International ran a small press campaign over two years which proved to be most successful and made its mark in what has become a fiercely competitive sector.

7.3   The results produced:

> Short-term profitability achieved by capitalising on membership. Research showed that this was perceived to be better 'value' for money than just giving donations. The member receives a magazine every two months and campaigning literature.
>
> Long-term profitability as members pay annual subscriptions and generally stay in the organisation for a number of years.
>
> Increased members recruited – 12 times higher per insertion than previous Amnesty advertising.
>
> A list of names for direct mail appeals and trading.
>
> Increased awareness of Amnesty International.

7.4   The advertising campaign took place in a very competitive environment. The total number of charities advertising and their total spend had increase dramatically but total voluntary income had barely increased. Telethons, disaster appeals etc were all fighting for a share of the public's mind and pocket. Research showed that Amnesty's closest competitors were Greenpeace, Anti-apartheid, Oxfam and Christian Aid.

7.5   The three marketing objectives of Amnesty International's fundraising department were, in order of priority:

> i.   to develop a large and active membership;
> ii.   to increase the groundswell of public support;
> iii. to generate funding for campaigning, organisation and international activities.

7.6   The tools involved to achieve these objectives included:

Advertising
Direct marketing
Trading
Direct campaigning
Local activities
Events
Media relations

7.7   Up until 1988, advertising played a small role in publicising and selling tickets for events such as *The Secret Policeman's Ball*. In June 1988, Amnesty International appointed an advertising agency to help meet its three marketing objectives.

ADVERTISING OBJECTIVES

7.8   A common sense definition of the target market was used:

younger men and women;
liberal minded people;
having a basic awareness of Amnesty and current affairs;
readers of *The Guardian, The Independent, The Observer*.

Subsequent research showed that members tended to be educated, young, liberal, professional and middle class.

7.9   Advertising was aimed at recruiting new members from this section, assuming a greater tendency to join among this group and, through experience, *The Guardian* elicited a higher response than *The Sunday Mirror*. A time will come when this group is no longer profitable to target and the long-term objective was to recruit from a broader base. In the short-term, however, it was necessary to maximise profit and advertising further afield was restricted to free space.

THE CAMPAIGN

7.10   Where possible, direct response data was supplemented by small qualitative programmes of research, often conducted at no cost to Amnesty.

7.11   It was decided that the advertising should focus on the problems Amnesty handled. Anyone reading the papers is confronted by a barrage of similar charity advertising, so impact rests on having a verbal or visual hook. Due to the horrible nature of what Amnesty deals with – torture, hanging, sexual abuse – there is the risk of deterring readers' involvement. Therefore, a more symbolic approach was adopted where the full horror of the situation is lurking just below the surface.

7.12   The advertising had mostly recruited members aged 22-24, who generally felt that they did not do enough 'worthwhile' things and chose Amnesty for a chance to feel 'involved' rather than 'just throwing money at the problem'.

7.13   In recruiting members, the ignorance of issues had to be overcome plus the feeling among non-members that Amnesty was an 'organisation' and 'far from home and real life'.

7.14   The advertising, therefore, needed to affect people personally and make them identify with the victims rather than just setting out Amnesty activities.

ADVERTISING DEVELOPMENT

7.15   *Letters*

Realistic translations of real letters from prisoners spoke for themselves and hopefully achieved a very personal communication with readers. It also built on any existing awareness of the Amnesty letter-writing activities.

7.16   *Death Penalty*

New advertising was developed to coincide with a major Amnesty publicity campaign against the death penalty. Photographs were chosen to be visually compelling with headlines bringing out the barbaric nature of execution.

7.17   *China*

An advertisement was prepared using an existing visual (*Times* cartoon) following the Tiananmen Square massacre.

7.18   *Bazoft*

Two advertisements were used at the time of Bazoft's execution in Iraq. The first was all text (for speed), the second using the noose photography followed two days later.

MEDIA

7.19   To stand out from the usual 20 x 2 column size charity advertisements, Amnesty used 25 x 4 column. More space was needed to create the impact and communication required, given the low level of knowledge about Amnesty.

Advertising budget available	1988	£30,000
	1989	£50,000
	1990	£150,000

The bulk of the money was spent on core publications – *The Guardian, Independent* and *Observer*. In many cases, the smaller publications offered free space.

7.20 Publicity had an effect on response as shown here:-

EFFECT OF HEAVY PUBLICITY IN 1988
(Running the same advertising)

June/Oct 1988	Average Response (Members)	*Observer*	119	
		Independent	122	
		Guardian	98	
Dec. 1988	Average Resonse	*Observer*	207	(+ 74%)
		Guardian	148	(+ 51%)
		Independent	182	(+ 49%)

Note: PR in Dec 1988: *Secret Policeman's Third Ball,* TV screening of *Amnesty World Tour* and TV series on human rights.

7.21 While some of this effect might have been cumulative, i.e. the campaign wearing in, other examples show that there is a genuine effect of advertising – which also works in reverse. The response in December 1989, when many people were upset at Amnesty's unpatriotic publicity about Hong Kong, shows a negative effect. Responses fell by an average 60 per cent in core publications, compared to previous exposure of the same advertisement.

RESULTS

	Inserts	Rate Card (£)	Actual Cost (£)	Production (£)	Total Spend	Recruits
Letters (Jun-Dec 88)	22	88,222	18,050	13,446	31,496	1852
Death Penalty (April 89)	5	15,250	10,400	3,930	14,330	780
Tiananmen (Jun-July 89)	4	23,742	13,200	2,532	15,732	510
Death Penalty (Aug-Dec 89)	8	26,047	14,300	2,323	16,623	903
Iraq (Mar 90)	8	25,510	1,000	3,058	4,058	673
TOTAL	47	178,771	56,950	25,289	82,239	4718

The effectiveness of advertising rests on media buying, as well as creative strength.

7.22 Some interesting points arise from the recruitment results.

1) Results for the Tiananmen ad fell well below standards set by previous advertising. Partly because the ad did not go to press until a week after the event. At that late stage, the agency had little leverage for cheap space with the press on the basis of topicality and public interest had fallen away.

2) In March 1990, with the above lesson learnt, the agency achieved the placement of an ad in the papers the day after Bazoft's execution. This approach paid off in pure responses per exposure; doubly so as nearly 90 per cent of the media cost was free. Additionally, accompanying donations reached nearly £2,000.

3) Smaller publications have often requested ads which they have run for free after seeing them in the national press.

4) The 4,718 new members were definitely recruited by advertising. The figure comes from returned coupons only available on ads. One could perhaps ask the question as to whether some people might have joined by other means had there been no advertising.

5) The graph below strongly suggests that advertising alone was responsible for its recruits and indeed it may have increased the effectiveness of other methods of recruitment, like direct mail.

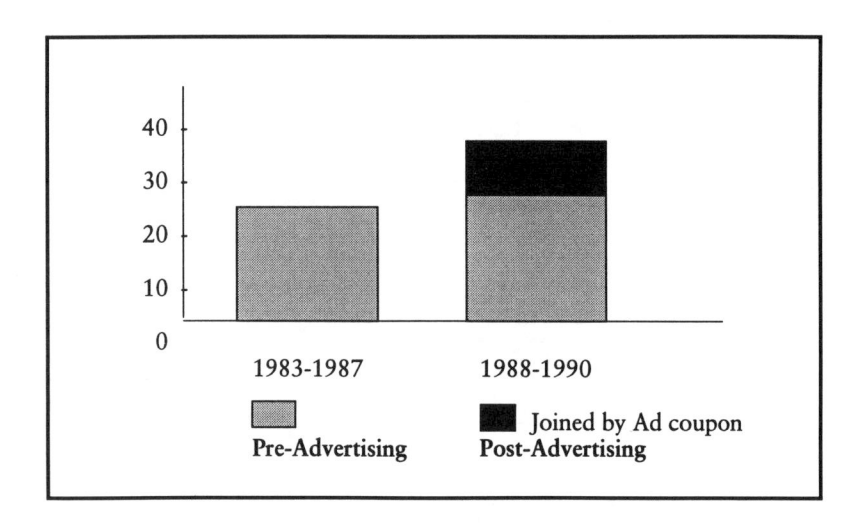

CONCLUSION BY THE ADVERTISING AGENCY

7.23 'The key to the success of our advertising was the recognition that membership offered a competitive edge and a long-term income. The whole paper has concentrated on how effective and creative advertising used these facts to secure a large profit for Amnesty International and, indeed, a larger profit than their previous advertising had generated. This gives a vary one-dimensional picture of what we have really achieved. Earlier this year, the agency had a visit from a man who had been arrested, imprisoned and tortured continuously for four years in Argentina. Letters from ordinary Amnesty members and visits from Amnesty delegates kept him going through his ordeal and, he believes, are the only reason he is alive and free today. If one member recruited by advertising wrote one letter that saved another human beings life – how could we possibly account for that on a balance sheet?'

Source: Information extracted from John Grant – BMP 'Advertising Works 6' – IPA Advertising Effectiveness Awards 1990.

Case Study: The Billy Graham Campaign

7.24 In 1989 FCB advertising agency was hired to handle the above-the-line support for Billy Graham Mission 89. Mission 89 organisation was a cross-section of Christians of all denominations who had invited Billy Graham to the United Kingdom. There were to be three major venues for the meetings, West Ham Football Stadium, Crystal Palace Athletics Stadium and Earls Court Arena. These meetings would be broadcast live by satellite to 250 venues in the UK, the Continent and Africa.

7.25 The aim of advertising was to raise awareness of the event so that the interest aroused could be used by various groups issuing individual invitations to the meetings. The tone was to be confident, contemporary, popular and intriguing.

7.26 Consumer research was carried out among four groups of men and women aged 21-34 years. Previous large scale missions showed that younger people were more likely to respond to such events than older people. The respondents either had friends who were active Christians or had loose church connections through baptism, weddings, etc. Those who claimed not to believe in God or who were from another religion were excluded.

7.27 The research showed that those interviewed had little direct knowledge of Billy Graham but they were aware that he was somewhat of a folk hero. They expressed interest in going to hear him because of who he was and because they expected him to be interesting. Although they knew he was trying to persuade people that Christianity was right, any advertising that mentioned God or which was too confrontational would antagonise them and cause rejection.

7.28 ADVERTISING STRATEGY

The problem for the advertising agency was that advertisements had to stand out within the clutter of a cynical and distracting city. The subject of the campaign was a low interest category where it was easy to offend people and make them switch off from the message.

7.29 THE TARGET GROUP

The target group would be all adults but primarily those in the 18-40 year age group. These would have previous contact with the Church through funerals or baptisms and weddings but would feel church was boring and irrelevant to everyday life. They would believe that God exists and that Christianity and the Bible are essentially true; but would claim to have no experience of God.

7.30 THE ADVERTISING TASK

There were two stages to the campaign. Stage one was intended to generate interest and build curiosity, creating awareness that an exciting event was about to happen. The second stage was to provide details of when and where Billy Graham was speaking.

7.31 THE ADVERTISING BRIEF

This had four aspects. The first aspect was to create advertising that was interesting in itself and would get talked about. The second was to proclaim that Billy Graham, a legend in his time, was coming to town. The tone was to be confident, contemporary, popular and intriguing. Last, Billy Graham did not necessarily have to be mentioned at the first stage.

7.32 THE MEDIA

It was decided to use posters and press advertisements. The posters would be 48 sheet, Superlites (lit bus stop posters) and 16 sheet cross tracks (the large posters across the tracks in Underground stations). Advertising would be focused within a two-month period: stage one in May and stage two in June. The campaign would be a heavyweight one. achieving 95 per cent coverage and 59 OTS (opportunities to see) of all adults in the London ITV area. The press would be targeted in June at 86 per cent coverage and 6.2 OTS.

The total budget - £392,700 posters, £191,600 press.

7.33 MEASURING THE IMPACT OF THE CAMPAIGN

The effect was measured in three ways:
    i.   Awareness of the event and the advertising.
    ii.   The number of people attending.
    iii.   The news coverage generated by the campaign itself, as opposed to general public relations.

7.34 AWARENESS

	Pre %	End Teaser %	Post %
Spontaneous Recall of Advert for Billy Graham	11	13	60
Prompted Recall of Advert for Billy Graham	12	17	72
Seen Teaser (Visual Prompt)	3	44	67
Seen Reveal (Visual Prompt)	5	13	74
Total Advertising Awareness	20	51	85

Base: Total Sample 400 Adults *Source:* RSGB Omnibus

	Pre %	End Teaser %	Post %
Heard of Billy Graham	78	78	91
Knew Billy Graham was in London in June	21	25	81

Where heard about Billy Graham's Visit (Spontaneous)	
Posters	46
Advertising	25
TV	38
Leaflet through/someone at door	13

7.35. ATTENDANCE

West Ham reached 82 per cent capacity.

Crystal Palace broke previous attendance records on all three nights.

Earl's Court reached 97.6 per cent across the week.

In addition, due to the organisers being unable to fulfil requests for tickets at Earl's Court, an additional meeting was arranged for Wembley Stadium which 72,000 attended.

A further 817,000 people heard Billy Graham live by satellite.

7.36 PRESS COVERAGE

There was considerable media coverage about the campaign with many national papers carrying articles about the advertising both before and after the reveal.

Thames TV, BBC1 South East and many radio stations carried news items about how the campaign was developed.

Finally, it was named Campaign of the Year by *Campaign* magazine.

Case Study: Oxford Diocese Christmas Campaign

7.37   In 1991, the Diocese of Oxford ran a small advertising campaign designed to encourage people to come to church at Christmas. Aspects of the campaign were taken up by about five other dioceses and the campaign was followed in 1992 by a second campaign, this time run by Oxford on behalf of the Churches' Advertising Network, with a much larger reach. The 1991 campaign is used as a case-study to see where it fits, and where it fails to fit, the criteria we have provided.

7.38   The first test of any campaign is whether it fits a larger communications strategy. In 1990, the Communications Committee of the Oxford Diocese reflected on its task in the light of the Decade of Evangelism. Recognising that the diocese already spent time and resources on internal communications, it made a commitment during the Decade of Evangelism to spend a larger proportion of its time and resources on reaching those who were not currently members of a church. An informal audit of its communications showed that, whilst it was using public relations skills effectively and a number of parishes were implementing programmes to reach those outside their membership, there was little evidence of any major initiative to use professional communications media to reach those completely outside the church's traditional reach.

7.39   Coincident with these considerations, a television programme on 'church-going' contained an interview with a young couple shopping at a supermarket. The interviewer asked them why they had not thought of going to church. Their answer was fascinating: 'You don't see it advertised much, do you?' Following these considerations, the diocese proposed a strategy for developing and testing an initial advertising campaign and, following an initial experiment with radio advertising before Easter 1991, the idea for the 1991 Christmas campaign was born.

7.40 The Communications Officer set three criteria for the campaign. First, it was to be created by a professional advertising agency. Given that there was a steep learning curve to be climbed, it was essential that the diocese should be guided by the professional expertise available through an agency.

7.41 Second, the campaign should not be denominational. The reasons for this were both to avoid any sense of competition between denominations and also to recognise that the target audience would interpret 'church' in a way that reflected their own history and preferences. It was believed that, by giving people a choice, there would be less sense of coercion and a greater sense of invitation.

7.42 Third, there should be a Christian working on the account at the agency. The reason for this was that, having little experience of professional advertising, the diocese would need to rely heavily, at least in the early stages, on the advice of the agency and wanted someone who could understand the language and motivation of the Church from the inside.

7.43 There was one other consideration: the budget for the campaign was almost non-existent. It was unlikely that an agency could be afforded on the entire budget, let alone on a proportion of it which would leave sufficient for execution. It was at this point that a member of a Reading church, Francis Goodwin, who was a professional advertising consultant and who had assisted the diocese in another aspect of its communications, offered his help. His advice was to spend the budget on getting the message right and to leave the cost of execution to be found from other sources.

7.44 The Institute of Practitioners in Advertising had offered the names of several companies which might help with a campaign on a cost-only basis. John Hollens, Managing Director of Genesis RMS, part of the Watts Lord Advertising Group, was one of two companies that responded and his offer was gratefully accepted. This, together with the support of Francis Goodwin, meant that the diocese was professionally served on both sides of the client-agency relationship. Both Genesis and Francis Goodwin continue to work with the Churches' Advertising Network and the results underline the fact that there are many lay people who are both willing and able to assist the Church to an extremely high professional standard if only we will allow them.

7.45 The brief to the agency was very clear. The campaign was designed to reach families, with children of 11 years or under, who did not come to church regularly. The reason for this choice was integral to the decision to advertise at Christmas. The aim of the campaign was to reach those who had little or no current link with the church: and the one time in the year when the largest number of people in that category own a part of the Christian story is at Christmas. In aiming to reach families with young children, the campaign unashamedly reflected the widely-held belief that 'Christmas is for the children'. If that view, right or wrong, could be built upon, it would be effective. There was also a secondary target group: those who had a past link with some aspect of the Church's life.

7.46   The theology behind the campaign was, and continues to be, that people come to faith through contact with a local Christian community. Therefore, a campaign which would encourage people to make contact with their local Christian community would meet this criteria. The aim was clear but limited: to encourage people within the defined group to come to church once over the Christmas period. The campaign, therefore, relied on the local church to provide accessibility and effective follow-up.

7.47   The campaign created by the agency was the result of a process where a number of creative suggestions were offered to the diocese as client and a preferred route was chosen after consultation. This was then developed, in partnership with the diocese, until the final solution was agreed. The resultant poster, with its words: 'Give Jesus a Birthday present. Wrap up the kids and bring them to Church', gained immediate support from the vast majority of parishes to which it was sent. The poster is reproduced on page 43.

7.48   Despite the cost-only basis of the campaign's creation, the media choices were severely constrained by the budget. However, with co-operation from media owners and printers, a mix of radio advertisement, posters, car stickers and PR back-up was achieved. Many of the ILR stations in the diocese agreed to play the radio advertisement free of charge – one station, FOX FM, actually recording the advertisement for the diocese from a supplied script.

7.49   Posters, car stickers and artwork for parishes to use in their own publicity were distributed free of charge to each parish in the diocese. Tapes of two versions of a radio advertisement – weeks one and two – went to each independent radio station in the diocese.

7.50   If it has proved difficult to locate resources to execute these campaigns, resources to research them have so far been non-existent. It is within this context that, after Christmas 1991, a student from St Stephen's House, who had professional experience of statistical research, gave time to run an evaluation of the campaign. Questionnaires were sent to 150 clergy across the diocese, asking them to rate the campaign themselves, by a number of criteria, and to reflect their congregation's view of the campaign. The questionnaire asked for numbers attending Christmas services in 1990 and 1991 and also for any anecdotal evidence of the effect of the campaign. This admittedly crude measurement showed not only that the campaign had been effective in reaching its targeted audience but that it had also been effective in gaining the desired response. Rough figures indicated that the campaign had been a contributory factor in an average 17.5 per cent increase in church attendance at Christmas services in 1991 over 1990. By any standard, this is a dramatic increase and the diocese was quick to point out that many other factors could be at work.

7.51   The 1991 campaign was followed in 1992 by a campaign commissioned and run by the newly-formed Churches' Advertising Network. Its results are relevant to this case study for several reasons.

GIVE JESUS A BIRTHDAY PRESENT.
WRAP UP THE KIDS AND BRING THEM TO CHURCH.

✝

REMEMBER WHAT IT'S ALL ABOUT.
COME TO CHURCH THIS CHRISTMAS.

7.52   First, the 1992 campaign took the strategy forward in a number of ways. It used 150 billboard sites (48 sheets), donated by Maiden Outdoor and Mills & Allen, thereby increasing the impact of the campaign by a considerable factor. It increased the number of participants, giving a coverage of at least a third of the country; and it drew on the research results of the 1991 campaign. In so doing, it threw into sharp outline the issues of strategy.

7.53   Second, the measurement of the 1992 campaign was more thorough. A control group was chosen against which the campaign was measured and the main variable, the general decline or growth of church attendance underlying the results of the campaign, was removed. Additionally, it measured the attitude of participating clergy against the increases in attendance, thereby allowing measurement of the impact of localisation. It was clear from the results that those clergy who felt positive or very positive about the campaign achieved greater impact in their use of the campaign. The resulting 16 per cent increase in attendance for those local churches which used the campaign effectively against those which had no interest is not dissimilar to the 1991 results. Set against a near 10 per cent decline in attendance generally, they send a clear signal.

7.54   Third, the 1992 Campaign drew on the feedback from Christmas 1991, not all of which was, in hindsight, appropriate. For example, strong negative feelings were expressed about the concept of 'the family' and the 1992 campaign possibly over-reacted to this criticism by broadening the targeted audience to 'everyone'! There was also criticism of the emphasis on what we do for God, rather than what he did for us. Thus, the line 'Christmas. It's enough to bring anyone to their knees' was a corrective and particularly appropriate to Christmas in a recession. It required a visual approach, however, which used the religious symbolism of the Magi and which itself drew criticism from the Churches' liturgists, who asked why we were celebrating Epiphany in a Christmas campaign! One participant, reacting against this use of religious symbolism, asked for the camels to be removed. (See page 45 for the 1992 campaign poster.)

7.55   Grammar, or rather the lack of it, caused irritation in both campaigns. The originating diocese very quickly discovered its members distaste for the word 'kids'. The following year, many were not slow to inform the diocese that the correct grammar should be: 'Christmas. It's enough to bring anyone to his or her knees'.

7.56   This evaluation points to several issues that the churches will need to bear in mind in any advertising campaign. First, the need, where possible (and it is usually possible in even the most informal way) to pre-test the campaign. Even more important is the related need to bear in mind the audience for whom the campaign is intended. Neither the 1991 nor the 1992 campaign brief had church members as part of the target audience but it was perceived to be important not to alienate the church which had to own the campaign. Thus, the 1992 brief over-reacted to criticism from those for whom the 1991 campaign was never intended! While there is an important balance to be maintained between

CHRISTMAS.
IT'S ENOUGH TO BRING ANYONE TO THEIR KNEES

reaching the target audience effectively and producing a campaign that can be owned by the Church, the primary task of a campaign to attract those outside the Church's reach may well require both media and messages that sit uncomfortably with the prevailing religious culture.

7.57   Taken together, the evaluation of both 1991 and 1992 campaigns point to two conclusions. The first is that, quite clearly, these particular campaigns have achieved their limited aim of bringing people to church who otherwise would not have come. This kind of advertising works best when the local church uses it effectively, thereby localising a national or regional campaign. The second is that, set against the resources committed to measurement and market research by most major charities and commercial organisations, the Church has not even reached the starting gate.

7.58   The evaluation would not be complete without retelling two of the stories which followed the campaign. The first, as related earlier in this report, involves a DCO who received a telephone call from an irritated parent who, it seems, had obeyed the 1991 campaign by wrapping up her infant and taking it to the 8.00 am 1662 Prayer Book Communion on Christmas morning, only to find that other participants did not exactly welcome the tranquillity of 'their' Christmas morning service being broken by the intrusion of a new baby. The second recalls the bishop who, some months later, was chatting to the newly confirmed and asked one couple what attracted them to the church. They told him they had responded to 'his' advertisement!

Chapter Eight Recommendations for the Churches

8.1 As we said at the beginning of this report, the Church has been advertising for a very long time. What we have been more concerned with is large-scale advertising, the coherent campaign, the utilisation of outlets with big audiences, a more sophisticated approach.

8.2 We believe that a Church of England strategy for communications is not yet shared and owned by all the dioceses. Since the communication of the Christian Gospel is of paramount importance, we find this state of affairs to be a matter for deep regret. We recommend that the Communications Unit takes the lead in this matter.

8.3 We believe that the Churches together have no common, agreed strategy for their joint communications. We recommend that the Church of England takes the initiative to work with other Churches in the development of such a common strategy forthwith.

8.4 We believe that advertising can be a creative, effective, appropriate, even amusing means of communication for the Church. We recommend that advertising be considered as part of the communications mix.

8.5 We believe that advertising can carry dangers for individuals, family units and societies. We recommend that, in addition to meeting the requirements of the regulatory codes, church advertising be conducted with sensitivity, responsibility and in accordance with Christian principles.

8.6 We believe that the Church gives far too low a priority to its thinking and budgeting on reaching those who do not hear its message. We recommend advertising be considered as one medium which may reach a broad spectrum of society.

8.7 We believe that the ecumenical approach is the right way for the Churches to use advertising on a large scale. We accept, however that individual Churches may wish, in some circumstances, to act on their own. We recommend that, in such cases, they inform their ecumenical partners before so doing.

8.8 We believe that, for any large-scale advertising, an agency needs to be hired. We recommend that it is made clear to any agency employed by or working for a Church that it should not use the relationship for the benefit of the agency, either through the agency's own advertising or in its client list. We also recommend that an agency's client list be checked to ensure that it does not include clients whose purposes are in conflict with the teachings or principles of the Church.

8.9 We believe that using advertising is a great responsibility. We recommend that it should only be used if considerable emphasis is given to resources and time is committed to thorough preparation, substantial research and subsequent evaluation.

8.10   We recommend that, while most campaign advertising on a national scale might be outside the financial capabilities of most Churches, to ensure a coherent and cost effective use of advertising, a user group be developed, taking the existing network as a basis and that Churches set aside money for this. This user group needs to be recognised by the General Synod and other similar Church bodies represented on the Group.

8.11   We believe that children can be at risk from advertising and that more research needs to be conducted into the effect of advertisements on children's behaviour and sense of values. We suggest that the Board of Social Responsibility and the Board of Education should carry this forward.

8.12   We recommend that the Radio Authority and the Independent Television Commission continue to offer guidance to the Broadcast Advertising Clearance Centre (BACC) on the interpretation of the rules for religious advertising and to monitor what is approved by the BACC.

8.13   We recommend that there should be a member with specialist knowledge of religious belief on the advertising committee of the Independent Television Commission, to which the Radio Authority also has access.

Acknowledgement

8.14   This Report would not be complete without paying tribute to those professional lay men and women who are already contributing in many ways to the growing use of effective advertising by the Church. Many give their time and their company's time, at considerable personal cost, to help the Christian community understand and use this medium more effectively. We have a great deal to learn still but this report might be a milestone on the journey.

Appendix A Members of The Working Party

Canon Colin Semper (Chairman)
Canon Treasurer of Westminster Abbey since 1987. Head of Religious Programmes for BBC Radio and Deputy Head of Religious Broadcasting, BBC, 1969-82. Provost of Coventry, 1982-87. Colin Semper is now a regular freelance broadcaster on a variety of channels, mostly radio.

Dr Richard Higginson
Director of The Ridley Hall Foundation for the Study of Faith and Work Issues, formerly the 'God on Monday' project. Lecturer in Ethics in the Cambridge Theological Federation and previously at St John's College, Durham. Dr Higginson is a lay theologian with a special interest in the world of business. He is the author of *Called to Account – Adding Value in God's World*, published by Eagle in June 1993.

Dr Jim McDonnell
Director of the Catholic Communications Centre. Previously, Director of Projects at the Centre for the Study of Communication and Culture, an international Jesuit centre promoting and facilitating research and consultancy projects on the church and the mass media. During the past few yearsl, Dr McDonnell has worked closely with the media offices of the British Churches, providing expert help in planning and co-ordinating ecumenical responses to the Government's proposed changes in broadcasting.

Miss Marilyn Sweetland
Marilyn Sweetland has been employed in the field of advertising since 1979. She has worked as an Account Manager with David Pilton Advertising since November 1987, when she was appointed to handle the ASTRA account, including all marketing aspects of satellite television in the UK. Additional clients include Steinway and Sons and The Cable Authority.

The Revd Richard Thomas
Diocesan Communications Officer for the Oxford Diocese since 1989. Diocesan Communications Officer for Winchester and Rector of All Saints, Winchester, 1983-1989. Richard Thomas has organised Christmas Advertising Campaigns 1991 and 1992 and co-ordinates the Churches' Advertising Network. He is also Chairman of the Churches' Media Trust and a Member of the Institute of Public Relations.

Consultant: The Revd Eric Shegog, Director of Communications for the Church of England. Former Head of Religious Broadcasting, the Independent Broadcasting Authority.

Secretary: Miss Andrina Barnden, Senior Secretary, the Communications Unit.

TERMS OF REFERENCE

That a working party be established with the following brief:

i. to consider what the Church of England's advertising policy should be, paying particular attention to ethical and theological considerations

ii. to consider the establishment of a Churches' Advertising User Group

MEETINGS

The working party met on six occasions and heard evidence from:
Kathy Phillips, Christian Aid,
Carolyn Woolrich, FCB (responsible for the Billy Graham Campaign),
Revd Robert Ellis, DCO Lichfield,
Revd Martin Field, Church Urban Fund.

Appendix B Codes of Advertising Standards and Practice

ITC

Introduction

1 These rules apply to advertising which is submitted by or on behalf of any body with objects wholly or mainly of a religious nature or which is directed towards any religious end. They also apply to advertising having a similar connection to systems of belief or philosophies of life which do not involve recognition of a deity but which can reasonably be regarded as equivalent or alternative to those which do. The term 'religious' where used below should be interpreted as also referring to this wider category. The terms 'advertisement' and 'advertising' here refer to all advertising subject to this Appendix.

2 All advertising subject to this Appendix must comply with the general requirements of the main Code as well as the detailed rules below. Attention is drawn particularly to Rule 10 of the main Code which prohibits advertising of a political character.

3 The Commission recognises that religious advertising on UK television is a relatively new departure which may require early review of rules drawn up largely on the basis of anticipation, rather than working experience of viewer reaction and advertisers' practice and intentions.

Acceptable Categories

4 (a) Advertising is acceptable for any of the following purposes:

    (i)   publicising events such as services, meetings or religious festivals;

    (ii)   describing an organisation's activities and how to contact it;

    (iii)   offering publications or promoting the sale or rental of other merchandise.

(b) Advertising which, while ostensibly for one of these purposes, appears to the Commission to conflict with other requirements of these rules or the general Code is not acceptable.

Unacceptable Advertisers

5 No advertising is acceptable from bodies:

    (i)   which practise or advocate illegal behaviour;

    (ii)   whose rites or other forms of collective observance are not normally directly accessible to the general public.

Fund Raising

6 (a) Subject only to (b) below, advertisements must not include appeals for funds.

(b) By prior arrangements, the Commission may exempt from this requirement advertisements from religious charities who can reliably demonstrate that any proceeds from television advertising will be devoted solely to the benefit of identified categories of disadvantaged third parties and that the conveying of such benefit will not be associated with promotion of any other objective (e.g. proselytising). Such advertising must also comply with the rules on charity advertising (Appendix 4 of the ITC's Code).

Doctrinal References

7 Advertising must not be used to expound religious doctrine. References to matters of doctrine or belief may only be incidental to advertising for one of the purposes in Rule 4 above and should not be expressed as unqualified assertions but in ways which make it clear to viewers that they represent the advertiser's belief.

Denigration

8 No advertisement may denigrate other religious faiths or philosophies of life. Claims to the effect that a particular religion is the 'only' or 'true' faith are not acceptable.

Use of Fear

9 No advertisement may play on fear. References to the alleged consequences of not being religious or not subscribing to a particular faith are not acceptable.

Benefit Claims

10 Any incidental references to the benefits of religion for personal well-being should be restrained in manner. Testimonials and references to individual case-histories are not acceptable.

Faith Healing and Miracle Working

11 No advertisement may promote faith healing or miracle working.

Counselling

12 Without the prior agreement of the Commission, no advertisement may offer to provide spiritual, moral or emotional counselling.

(Note: This Rule mirrors the prohibition on commercial services offering advice on personal or consumer problems in 18 (vii) of the main Code.

Children and Young People

13 (a) No advertisement for the purposes of 4(a)(i) or 4(a)(ii) above may be designed to appeal particularly to people under 18 and no advertisement may be broadcast in breaks in or immediately before or after programmes principally directed at audiences under 18 or likely to have particular appeal for such audiences.

(b) Advertisements for responsible, commercially available publications and merchandise based on religious themes and designed for children or young people may be broadcast in breaks in or adjacent to programmes for such people, provided the marketing of the products concerned is not ancillary to a recruitment or fundraising purpose.

Vulnerable Categories of Viewer

14 No advertisement may seek to exploit the vulnerability of any particular category of viewer (e.g. the elderly, the bereaved, or separated).

Free Offers

15 Advertisements may offer to send publications (including tapes and videos) free to enquirers but may not contain any other free offers.

Follow up to Advertising

16 Advertisers must be required to give the following assurances:

(i) that they will not publish or otherwise disclose names of respondents without their prior permission. Those organisations who hold their mailing list on computer must provide an assurance that they comply with the requirements of the Data Protection Act 1984 if they choose to publish or otherwise disclose the names of the respondents;

(ii) that they will not permit representatives to call on any respondent except by prior arrangement.

Acts of Worship

17 It is acceptable to show brief extracts of acts of worship but not in such a way as to conflict with any other requirement of these rules. Treatments which appear to involve viewers in an act of worship or prayer are not acceptable in advertisements.

Identification

18 All advertisements must clearly identify the advertiser or the religious organisation on whose behalf the advertisement is being broadcast.

Exhortations

19 Advertisements must not directly exhort viewers to change their religious behaviour.

Advertising on Specialised Religious Channels

20 The Commission recognises that differences between the characteristics and expectations of audiences who watch general channels and those who choose to watch specialised religious channels justify different rules for the latter on some of the matters referred to above. Details of certain relaxations to the rules for specialised religious channels are listed below. The Commission, however, reserves the right to apply or re-apply all or any of the rules should experience indicate this to be desirable.

Rule 4   The expounding of religious doctrine will be regarded as an acceptable purpose of religious advertising on such channels.

Rule 11 applies to such channels but advertising may, nevertheless, announce the times and venues of healing services and the like.

The following will not apply to such channels:

Rule 7   (Doctrinal References)
Rule 10 (Benefit Claims)
Rule 13 (Children and Young People). Advertising for products whose marketing is ancillary to a recruitment or fundraising purpose is not, however, acceptable.
Rule 17 (Acts of Worship). Acts of worship must not, however, be shown in such a way as to conflict with other requirements of the rules.

Note: For these purposes, a 'specialised religious channel' is a service licenced under Part I, sections 45 and 47 of the Broadcasting Act 1990 by virtue of a determination by the Commission under Schedule 2, Part II.2 (2) (a) of the Act.

Refusal to Broadcast Religious Advertising

21 Licensees who do not wish to carry religious advertising at all are free to adopt this policy. They may also impose such additional, generally applicable requirements as they consider necessary in the interests of viewers, provided these do not involve unreasonable discrimination either against or in favour of any particular advertiser.

This section of the ITC's code is published with permission.

RADIO AUTHORITY

These rules apply to advertising which is submitted by or on behalf of any body with objects wholly or mainly of a religious nature or which is directed towards any religious end. They also apply to advertising which is related to systems of belief or philosophies of life which do not involve recognition of a deity but which can reasonably be regarded as equivalent or alternative to those which do. The term 'religious' should also be interpreted as referring to this wider category.

All advertising subject to this Appendix must also comply with the general requirements of the Code, particularly Rule 8 which prohibits advertising of a political character and, in the case of religious charities, the rules of Appendix 5.

Advertisements in this category should be submitted for central copy clearance.

Rule 1 Refusal to Broadcasting Religious Advertising

Licensees who do not wish to carry religious advertising at all are free not to do so. They may also impose any additional generally applicable requirements they consider necessary in the interests of listeners, provided these do not involve unreasonable discrimination either against or in favour of any particular advertiser.

Rule 2 Acceptable Categories

The following categories may be advertised:

(a)   the publicising of events such as services, meetings or religious festivals;

(b)   the description of an organisation's activities and how to contact it;

(c)   publications or promotions for the sale or rental of other merchandise;

(d)   appeals for donations for charitable purposes.

(Practice Note: Advertising which, while ostensibly for one of these purposes, appears to the Authority to conflict with other requirements in these rules or the general Code is unacceptable).

Rule 3 Unacceptable Advertisers

No advertising is acceptable from bodies:

(a)   who practice or advocate illegal behaviour;

(b)   whose rites or other forms of collective observance are not normally directly accessible to the general public.

Rule 4 Identification

The name and denomination of a religious advertiser must be clearly identified in the advertisement concerned. Where a number of religious denominations advertise within a single advertisement, a generic identification is permitted provided that the faith which they share in common is made clear.

Rule 5 Children and Young People

(a) Advertisements by religious organisations for the purposes of 2(a), (b) and (d) above must not be designed to appeal particularly to people under 18.

(b) Advertisements for responsible, commercially available publications and other merchandise based on religious themes and designed for children or young people may be broadcast in or around programmes/features directed at children or young people, provided the marketing of the products concerned is not ancillary to a recruitment or fundraising purpose.

Rule 6 Distribution of Advertisements

Advertisements by religious organisations for the purpose of 2(a), (b) and (d) above must not be broadcast in or around programmes principally directed at people under 18, or likely to be of particular appeal to them (Please see Section A. Rule 2).

Rule 7 Appeals for Donations

(a) Religious organisations may advertise for funds or the donation of products/services for charitable purposes provided that:
  i. the organisation can reliably demonstrate to licensees that its *bona fides* are satisfactory;
  ii. the organisation can substantiate that donations will be carefully controlled, properly accounted for and devoted wholly to the purposes specified in the advertising;
  iii the advertisements identify the organisation/s and/or cause of the appeal and state how the donations will be used.

(b) Religious charities may advertise for funds or the donation of products/services provided that the advertising complies with all relevant rules of Appendix 5.

Rule 8 Doctrinal References

Advertising must not be used to expound religious doctrine. References to matters of doctrine or belief may only be incidental to advertising for one of the purposes in Rule 2 above and should not be expressed as unqualified assertions but in ways which make it clear to listeners that they represent the advertiser's belief.

Rule 9 Denigration

Advertisements must not denigrate other religious faiths or philosophies of life. Claims to the effect that a particular religion is the 'only' or 'true' faith are unacceptable.

Rule 10 Use of Fear

Advertisements must not play on fear. References to the alleged consequences of not being religious or not subscribing to a particular faith are unacceptable.

Rule 11 Benefit Claims

(a) Any incidental references to the benefits of religion for personal well-being should be restrained in manner.

(b) Testimonials and references to individual case-histories are unacceptable. This does not preclude the advertising of publications (including tapes and videos) which contain testimonials and individual case-histories.

Rule 12 Faith Healing

Advertisements must not promote faith healing or miracle working.

Rule 13 Counselling

Without prior approval of the Authority, advertisements must not offer to provide spiritual, moral or emotional counselling.

Rule 14 Acts of Worship

It is acceptable to broadcast brief extracts of acts of worship but not in such a way as to conflict with any other requirements of these rules. Treatments which appear to involve listeners in an act of worship or prayer are unacceptable in advertisements.

Rule 15 Exhortations

Advertisements must not directly exhort listeners to change their religious behaviour.

Rule 16 Vulnerable Categories of Listener

Advertisements must not exploit the vulnerability of any particular category of listener (e.g. the elderly, the bereaved or separated).

Rule 17 Free Offers

Advertisements may offer to send publications (including tapes and videos) free to enquirers but may not contain any other free offers.

Rule 18 Follow-up to Advertising

Advertisers must be required to give the following assurances:

(a) that they will not publish or otherwise disclose names of respondents without their prior permission.

(b) that they will not permit representatives to call on any respondent at his home or place of work except by prior arrangement made by correspondence or at the request of the respondent.

PRACTICE NOTE

Those organisations who hold their mailing lists on computer must provide an assurance that they comply with the requirements of the Data Protection Act 1984 if they choose to publish or otherwise disclose the names of the respondents.

SPONSORSHIP

Sponsorship of religious programming is permitted. Churches and other religious bodies may also sponsor programming.

These rules are published with the approval of the Radio Authority.

Appendix C Useful Contact Addresses

THE ADVERTISING ASSOCIATION
Abford House
15 Wilton Road
London SW1V 1NJ

Tel: 071-828 2771
General Public Enquiries: 071-828 4831
Fax: 071-931 0376

* Statistics, marketing pocket books, forecasts

ADVERTISING STANDARDS
AUTHORITY
Brook House
2/16 Torrington Place
London WC1E 7HN

Tel: 071-580 5555
Fax: 071-631 3051

* Complaints on print advertising

ASSOCIATION OF BRITISH MARKET
RESEARCH COMPANIES
c/o Research Support and Marketing
67 Caledonian Road
Kings Cross
London N1 9BT

Tel: 071-833 8251
Fax: 071-833 0993

ASSOCIATION OF MEDIA
INDEPENDENTS
48 Percy Road
London N12 8BU

Tel: 081-343 7779
Fax: 081-446 6794

ASSOCIATION OF INDEPENDENT
RADIO COMPANIES
46 Westbourne Grove
London W2 5SH

Tel: 071-727 2646
Fax: 071-229 0352

* Research, facts and figures

CABLE TELEVISION ASSOCIATION
5th Floor, Artillery House
Artillery Row
London SW1P 1RT

Tel: 071-222 2900
Fax: 071-799 1471

CINEMA ADVERTISING
ASSOCIATION
127 Wardour Street
London W1V 4AD

Tel: 071-439 9531
Fax: 071-439 2395

COMMITTEE OF ADVERTISING
PRACTICE
Brook House
2/16 Torrington Place
London WC1E 7HN

Tel: 071-580 5555
Fax: 071-631 3051

INCORPORATED SOCIETY OF
BRITISH ADVERTISERS
44 Hertford Street
London W1Y 8AE

Tel: 071-499 7502
Fax: 071-629 5355

INDEPENDENT TELEVISION
NETWORK CENTRE
200 Grays Inn Road
London WC1X 8HF

Tel: 071-843 8000
Fax: 071-843 8158

INDEPENDENT TELEVISION
COMMISSION
33 Foley Street
London W1P 7LB

Tel: 071-255 3000
Fax: 071-306 7800

INSTITUTE OF PRACTITIONERS
IN ADVERTISING
44 Belgrave Square
London SW1X 8QS

Tel: 071-235 7020
Fax: 071-245 9904

INSTITUTE OF PUBLIC RELATIONS
The Old Trading House
15 Northburgh Street
London EC1V OPR

Tel: 071-253 5151
Fax: 071-490 0588

JOINT COMMITTEE FOR
REGIONAL PRESS RESEARCH
Bloomsbury House
74/77 Great Russell Street
London WC1B 3DA

Tel: 071-636 7014
Fax: 071-631 5119 or 071 436 3873

JOINT INDUSTRY COMMITTEE
FOR NATIONAL READERSHIP
SURVEYS
44 Belgrave Square
London SW1X 8QS

Tel: 071-235 7020
Fax: 071-245 9904

ADVERTISING AGENCY REGISTER
26 Market Place
London W1N 7AL

Tel: 071-437 3357
Fax: 071-323 1321

* Supply of advertising agency showreels for a fee

THE MARKET RESEARCH SOCIETY
15 Northburgh Street
London EC1V OAH

Tel: 071-490 4911
Fax: 071-490 0608

ADVERTISING STANDARDS
AUTHORITY FOR IRELAND
IPC House
35/39 Shelbourne Road
Dublin 4

Tel: 010 353 16 608766
Fax: 010 353 16 608113

INSTITUTE OF ADVERTISING
PRACTITIONERS IN IRELAND
35 Upper Fitzwilliam Street
Dublin 2

Tel: 010 353 16 765991/764876
Fax: 010 353 16 614589

PUBLIC RELATIONS INSTITUTE
OF IRELAND
62 Merrion Square
Dublin 2

Tel: 010 353 16 618004
Fax: 010 353 16 764562

RADIO AUTHORITY
Holbrook House
14 Great Queen Street
London WC2B 5DG

Tel: 071-430 2724
Fax: 071-405 7062